On The Farm

An Adult Coloring Book

by

Donna Cook

Pen It! Publications, LLC

© 2017

ISBN #:   978-1547224876

ISBN #:   1547224878

Illustrated by: Donna Cook

First Edition © 2017

Pen It! Publications, LLC
penitpublications@yahoo.com
www.PenItPublications.com
www.BuyMeBooksNow.com

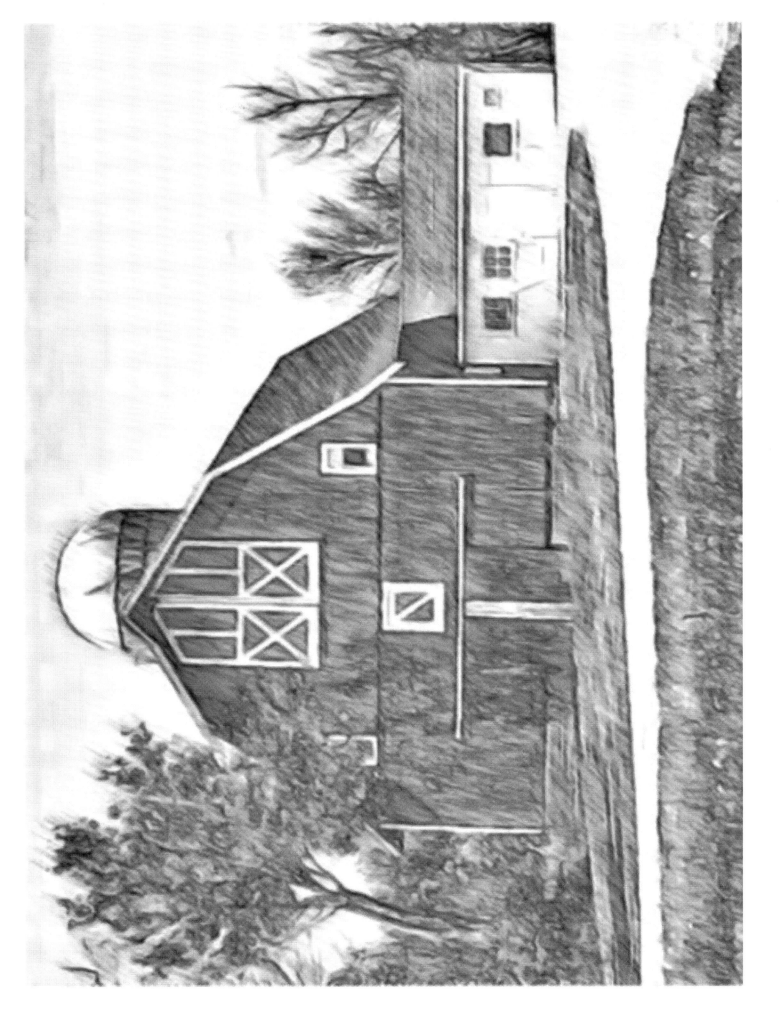

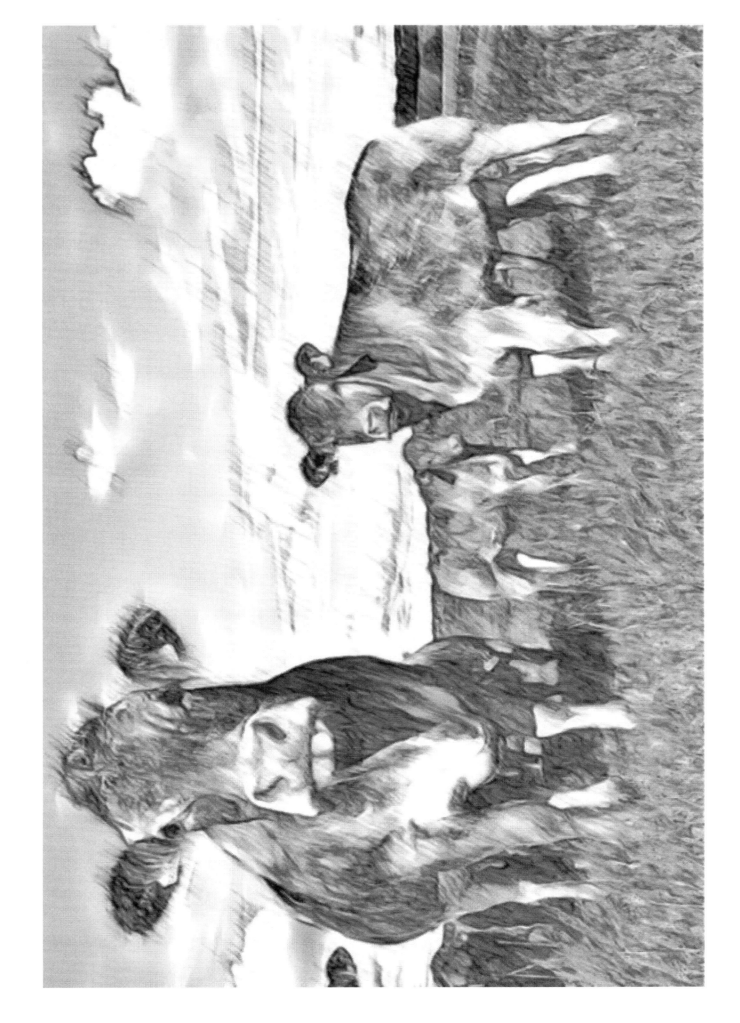

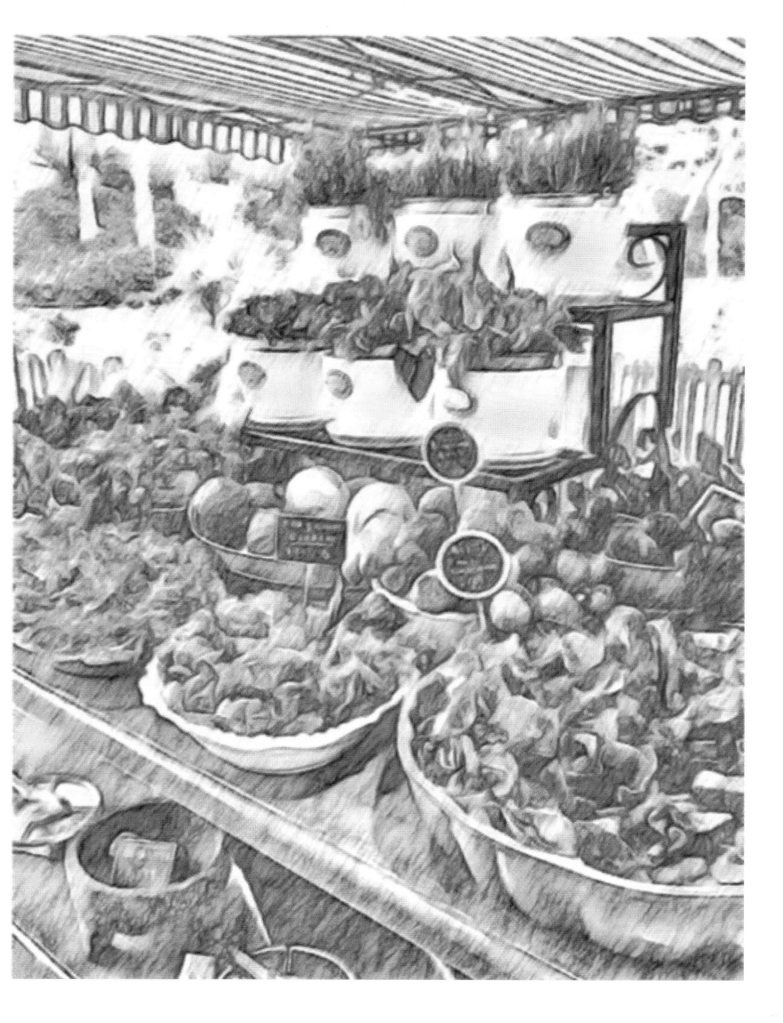

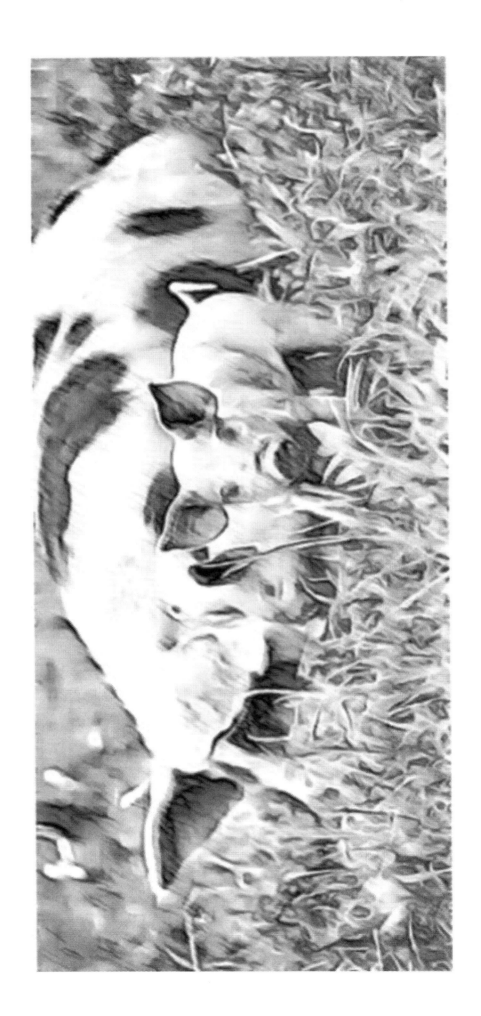

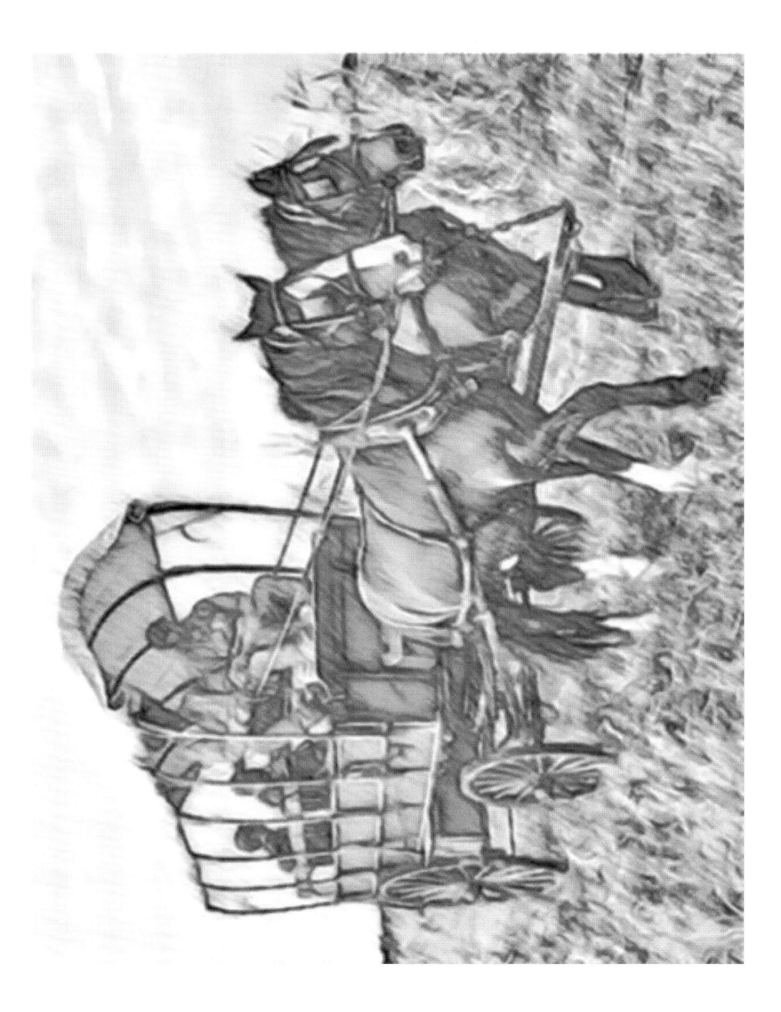

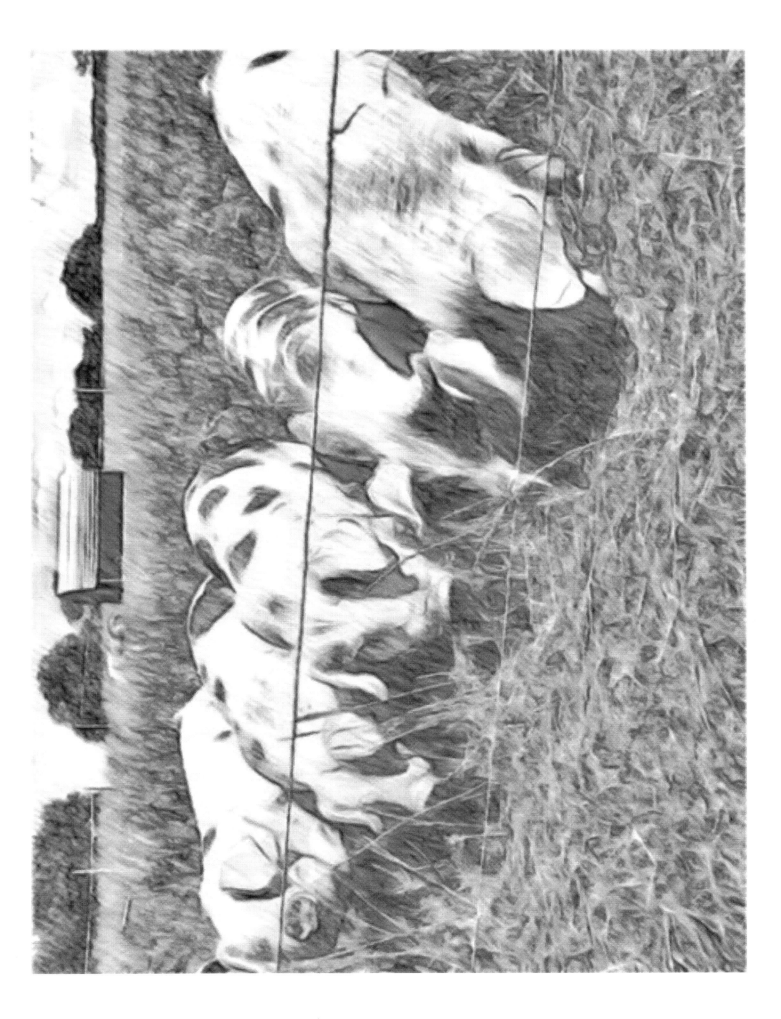

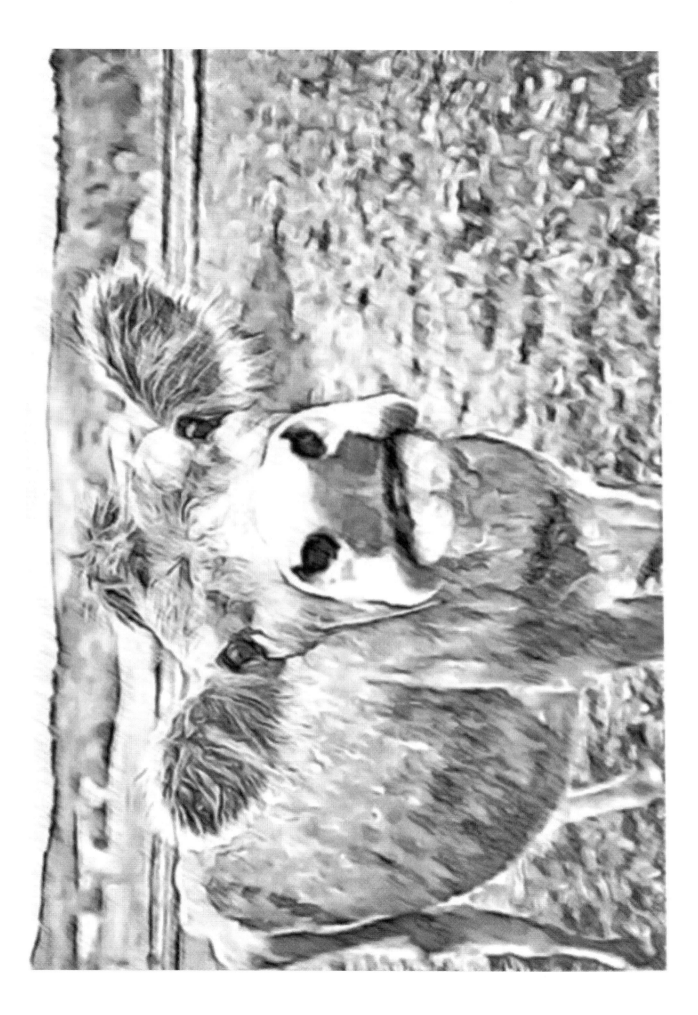

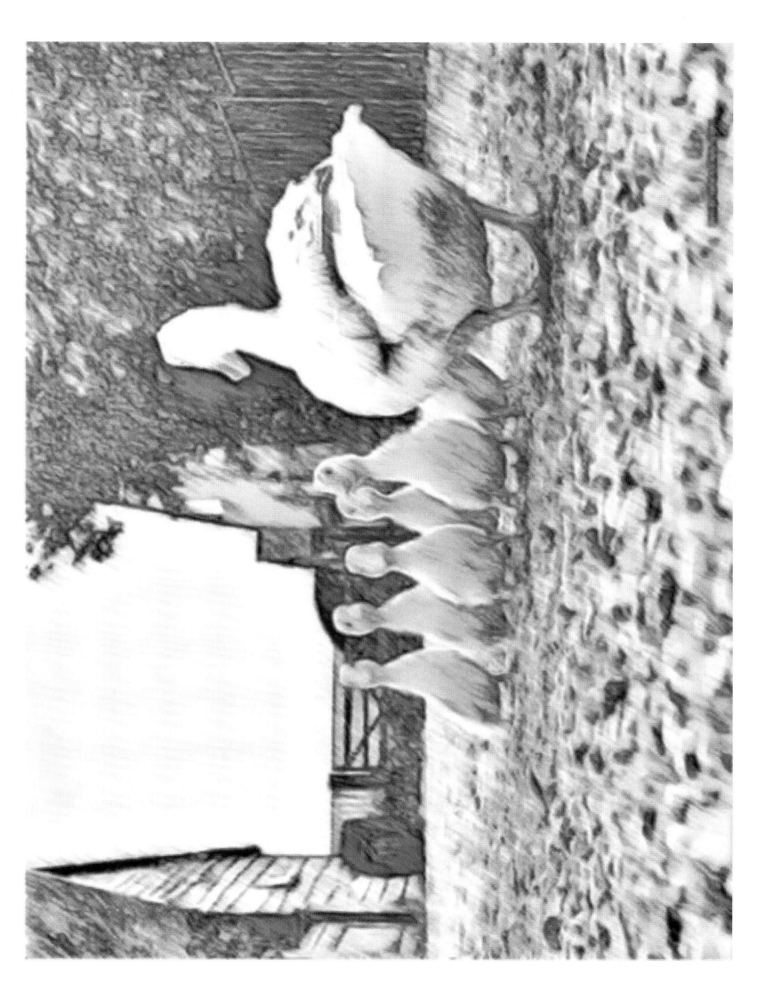

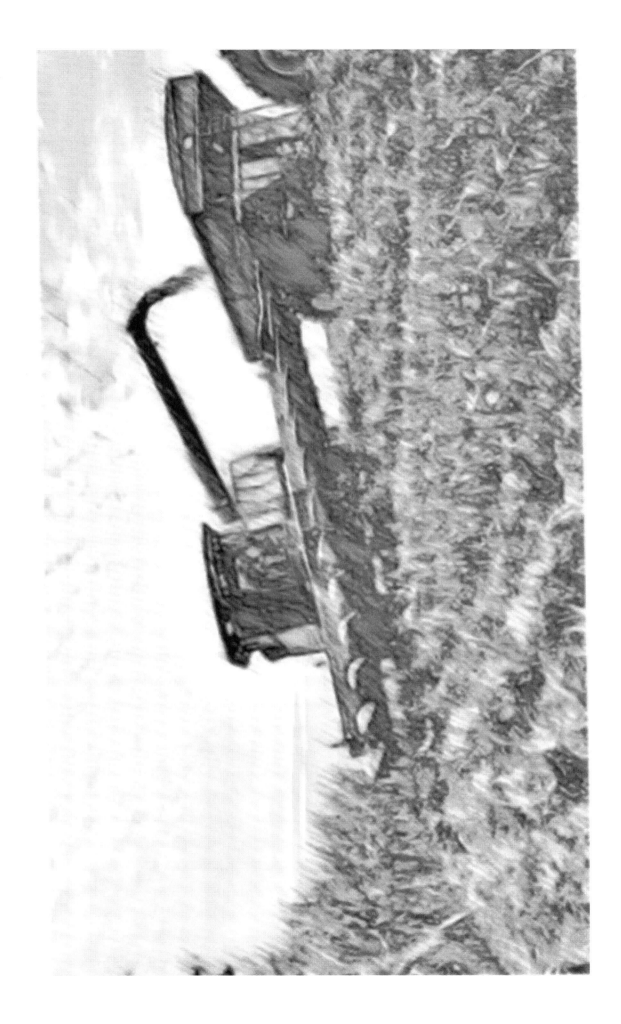

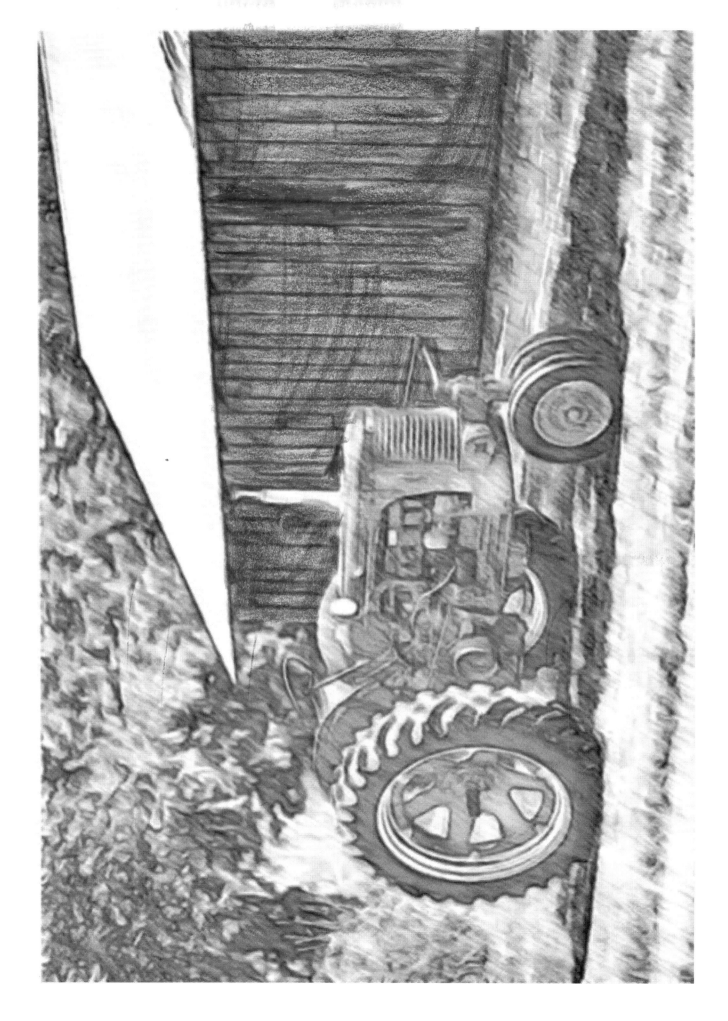

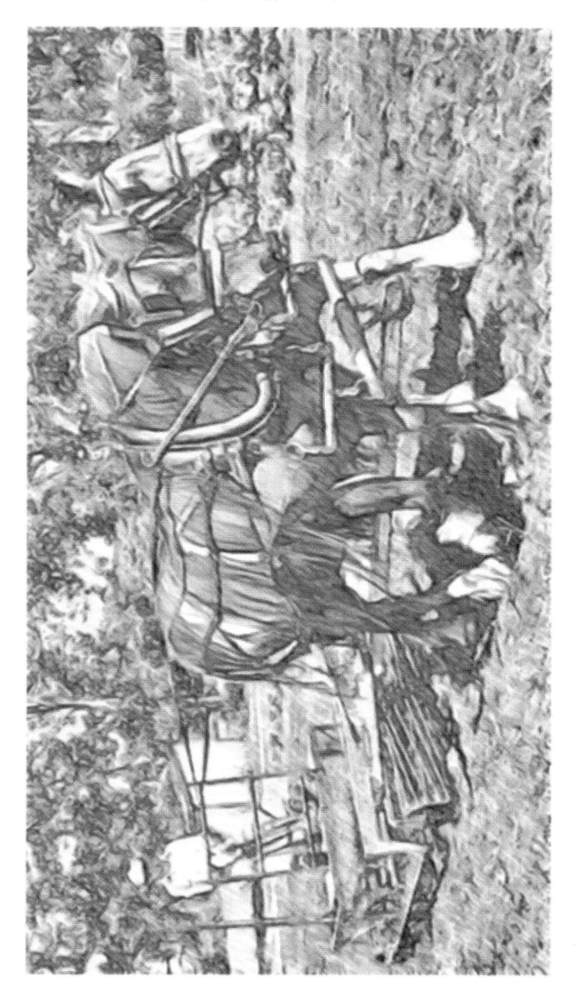

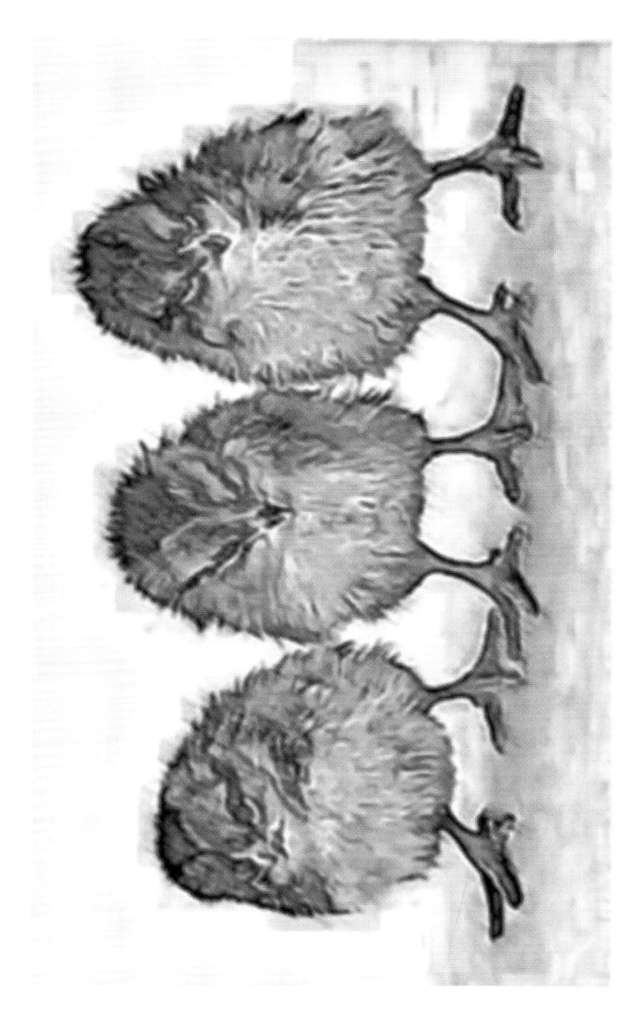

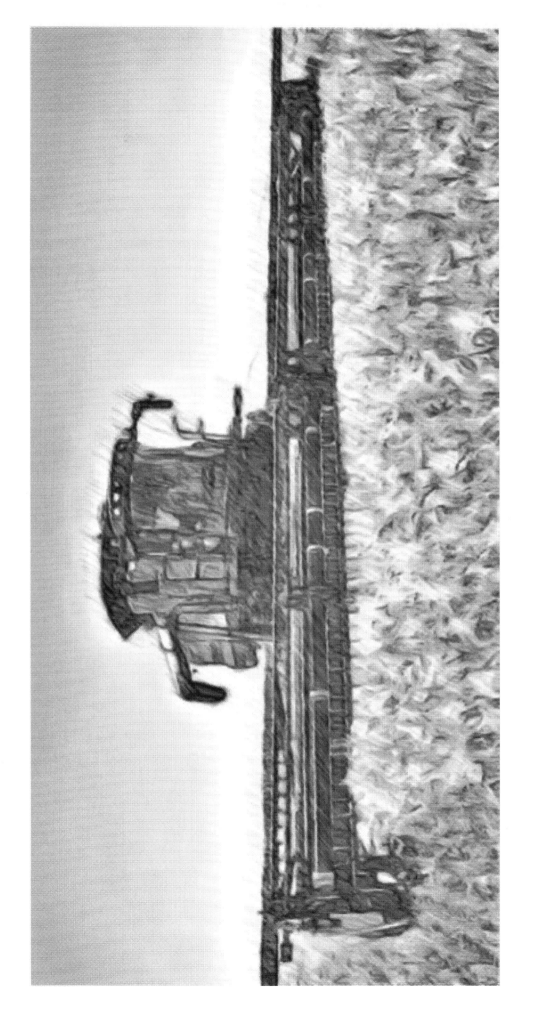

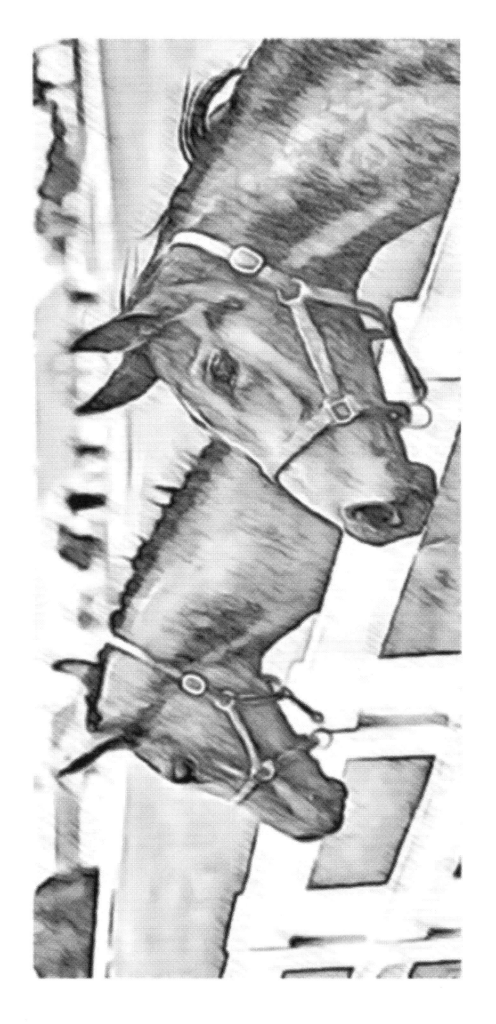

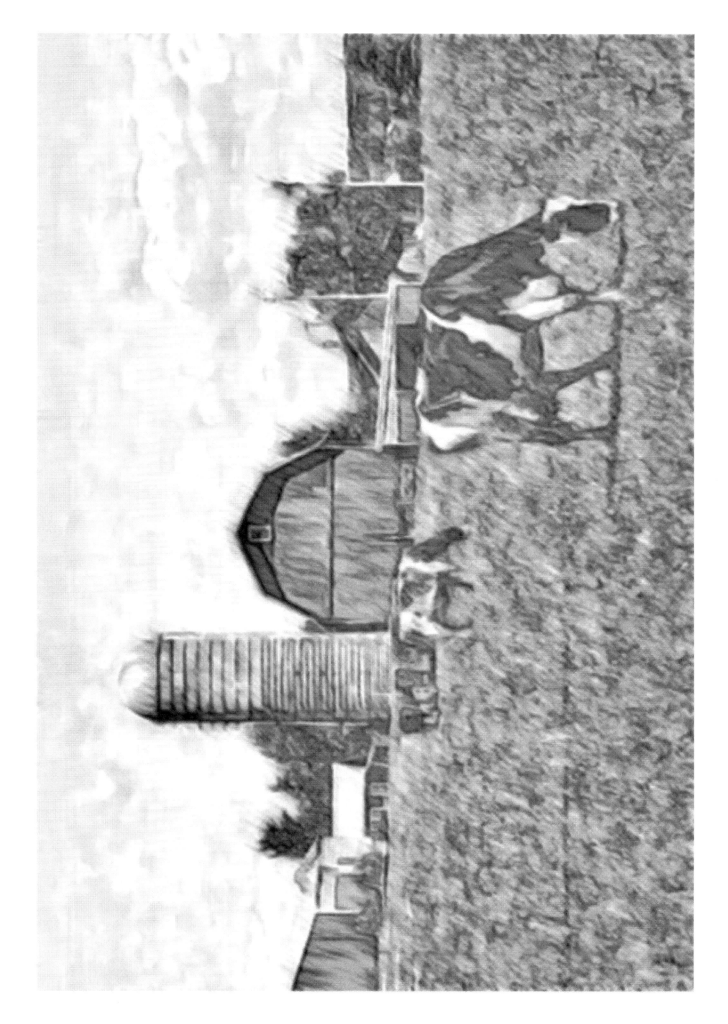

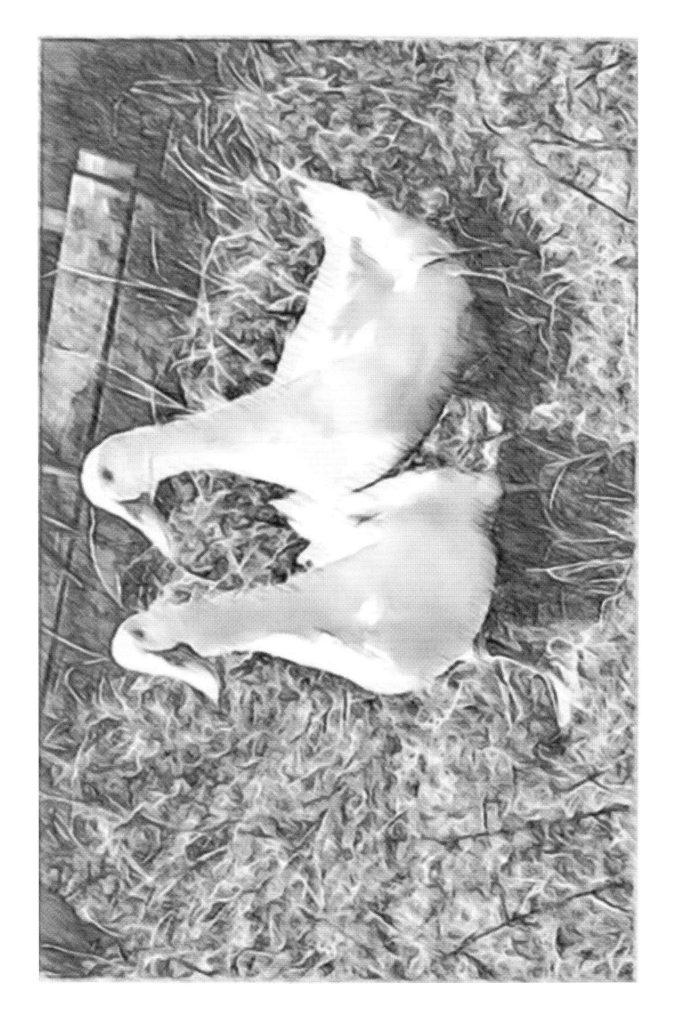

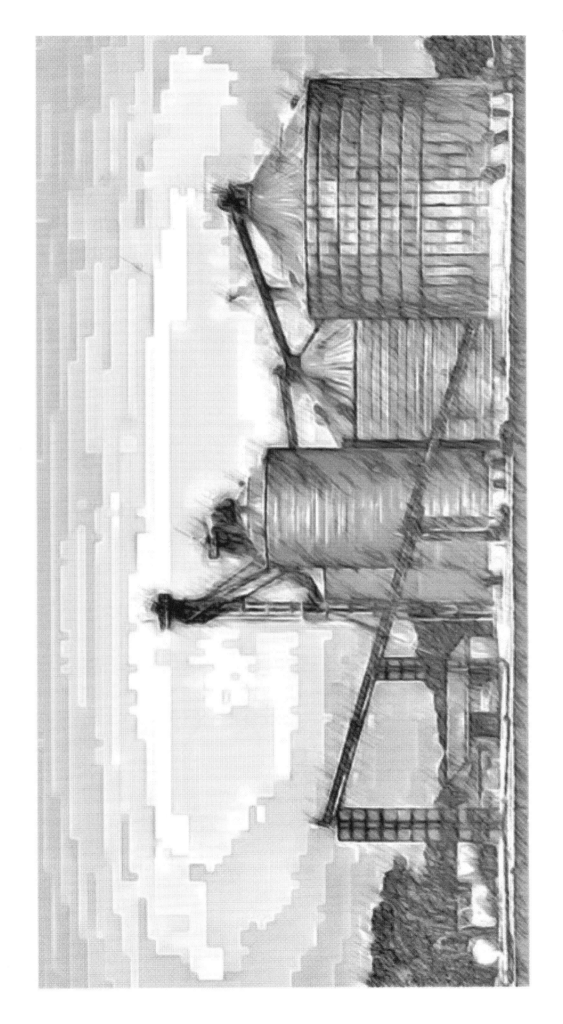

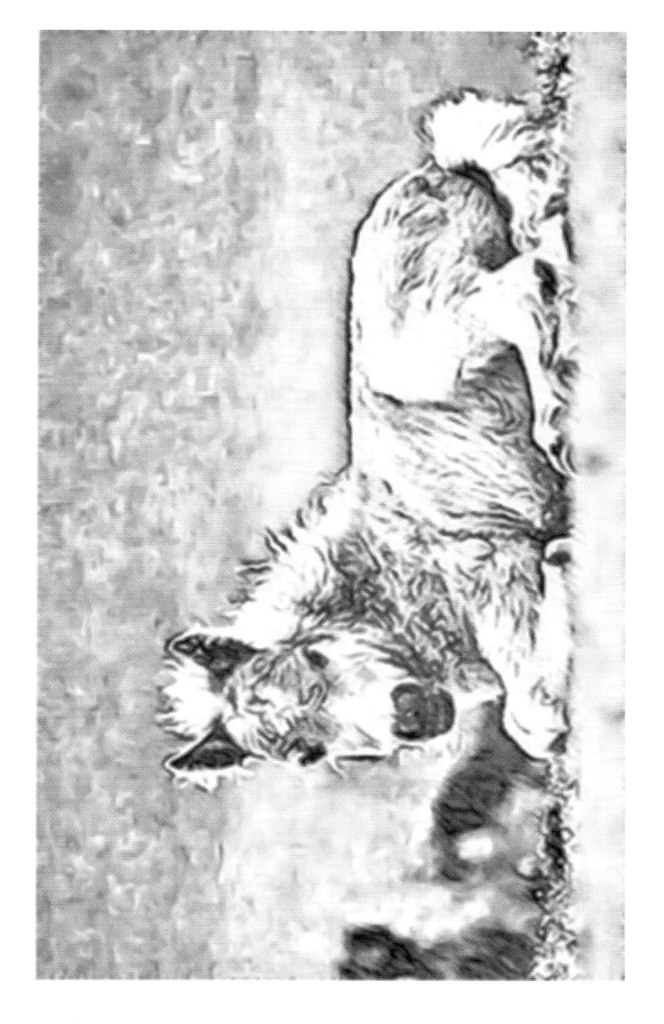

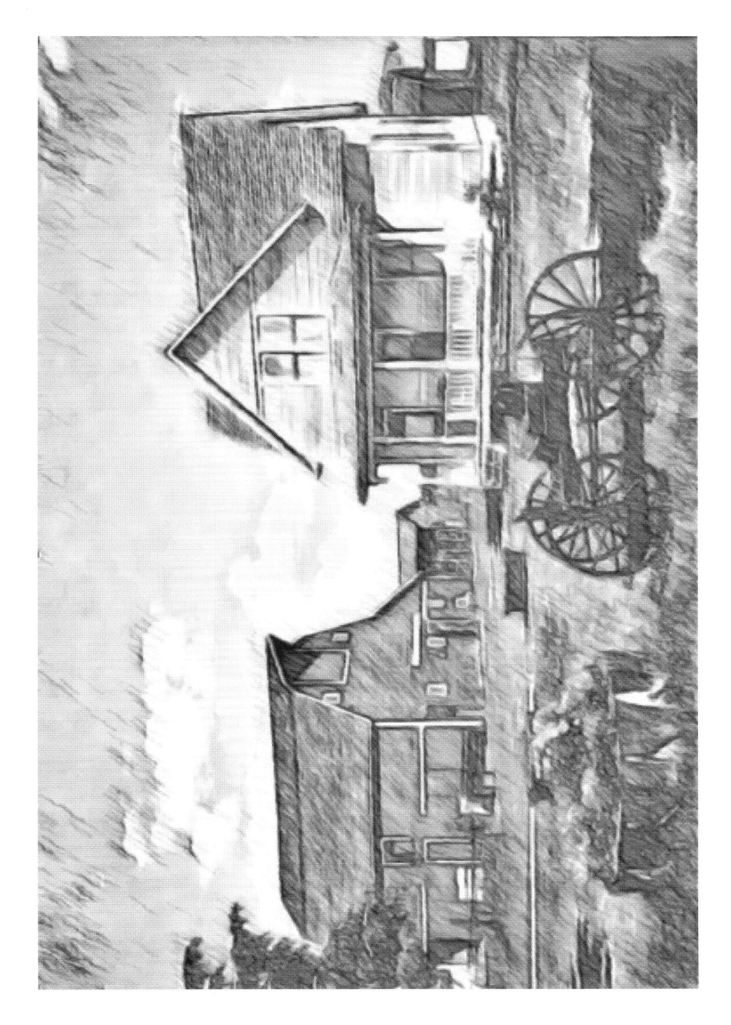

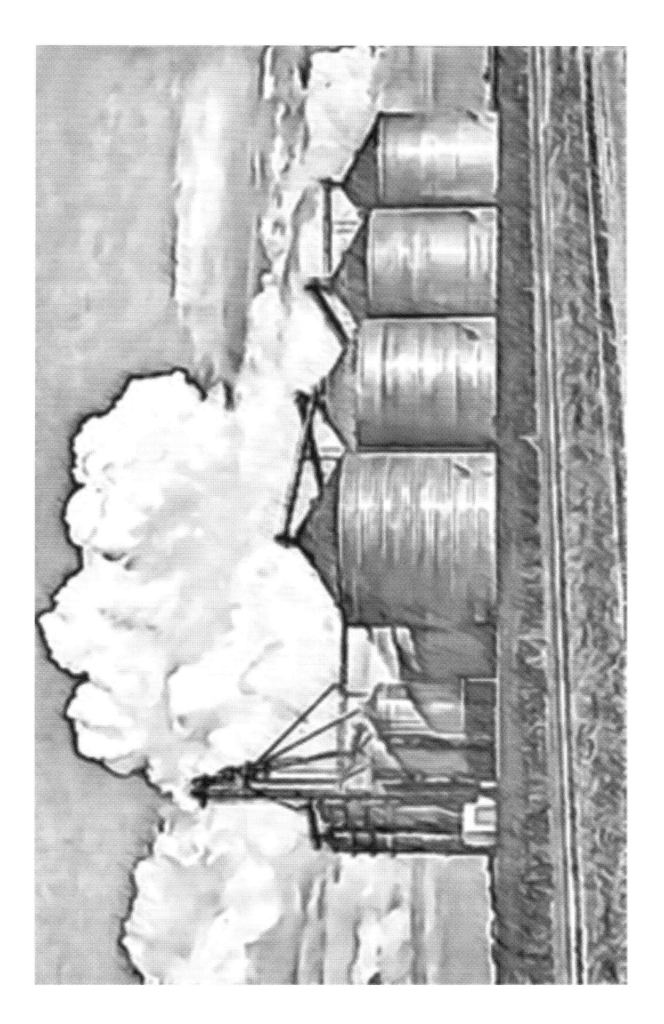

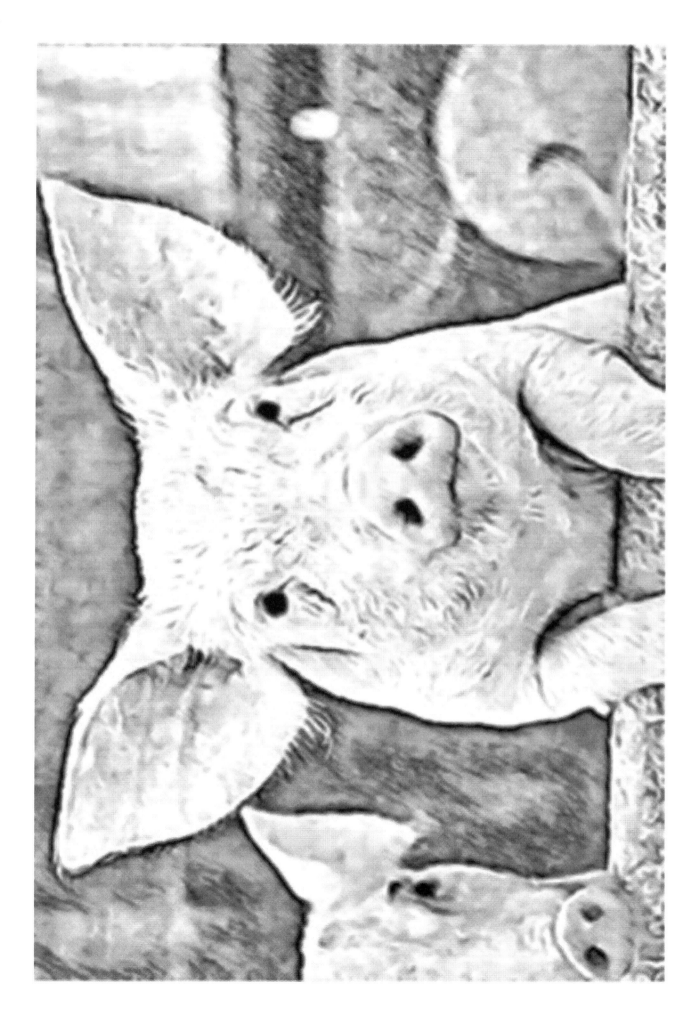

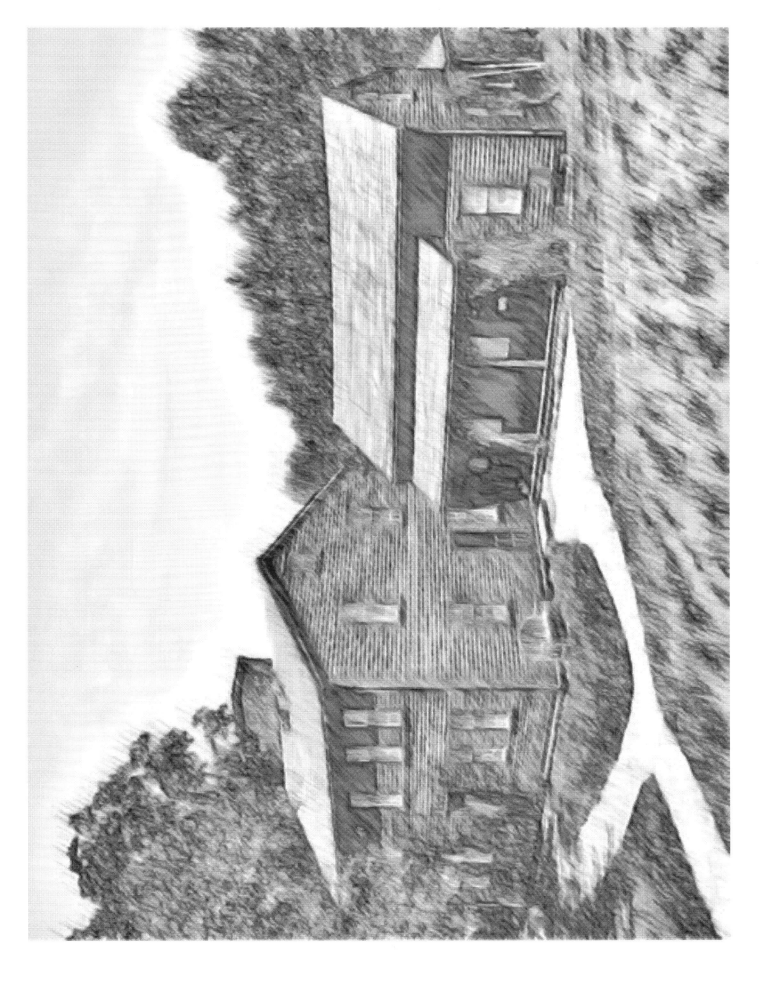

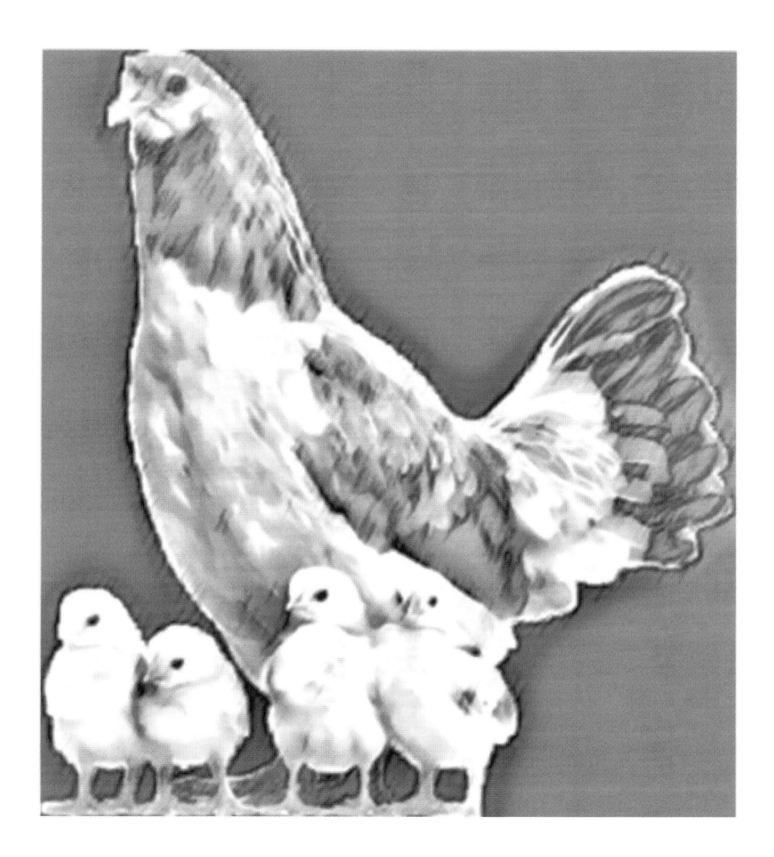

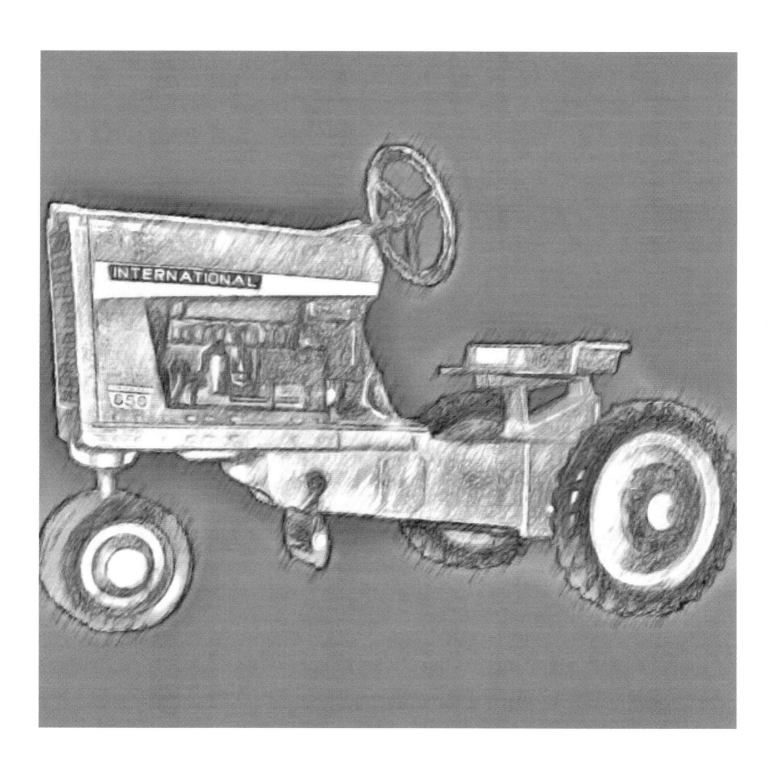

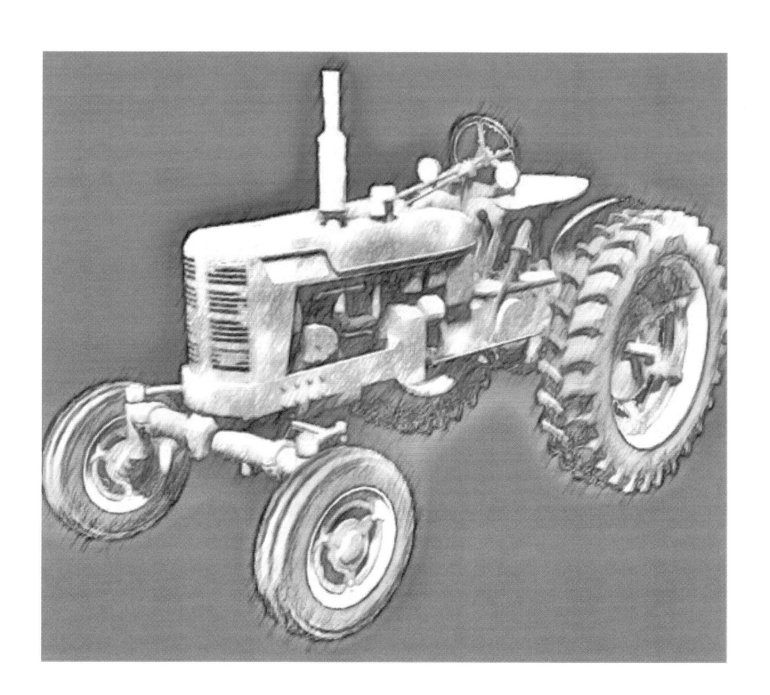

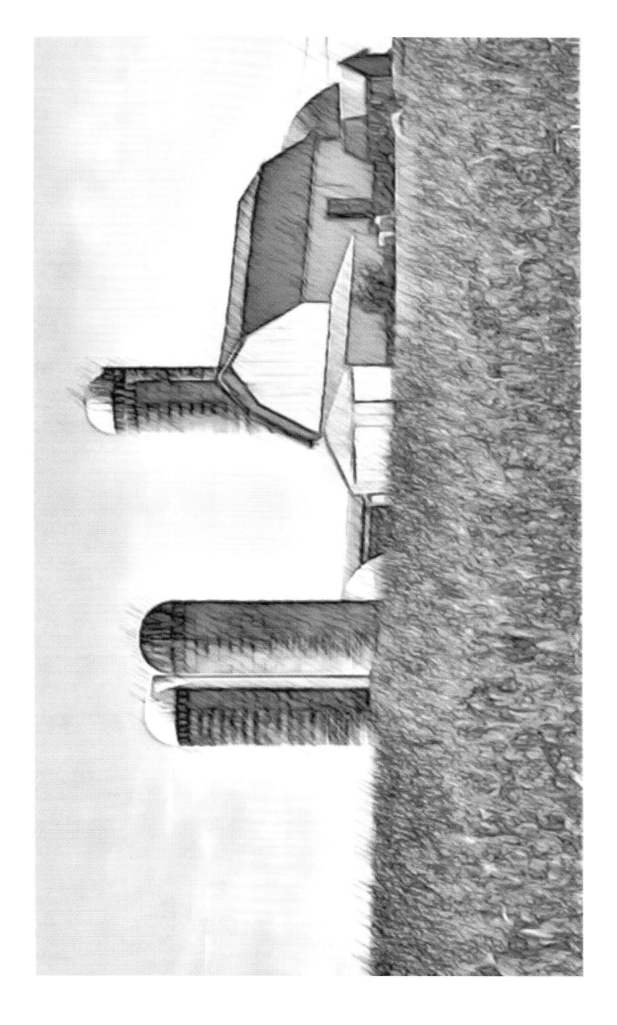

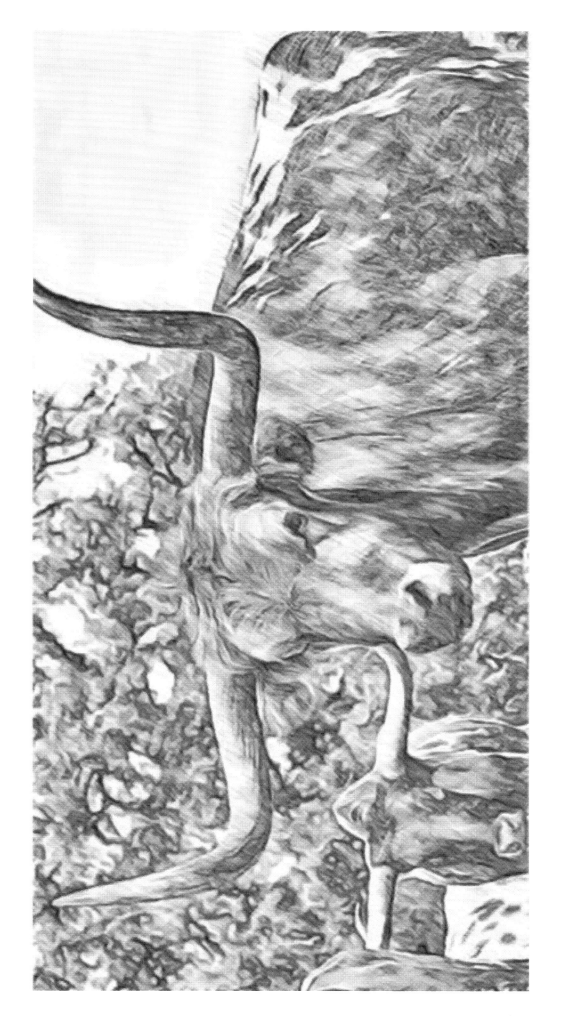

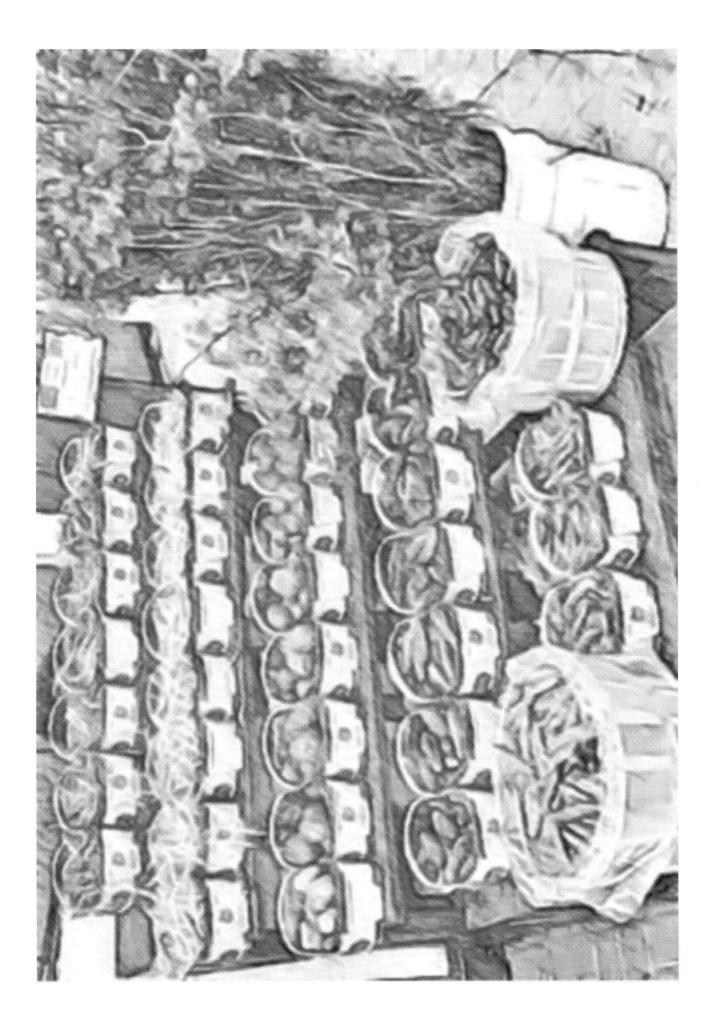

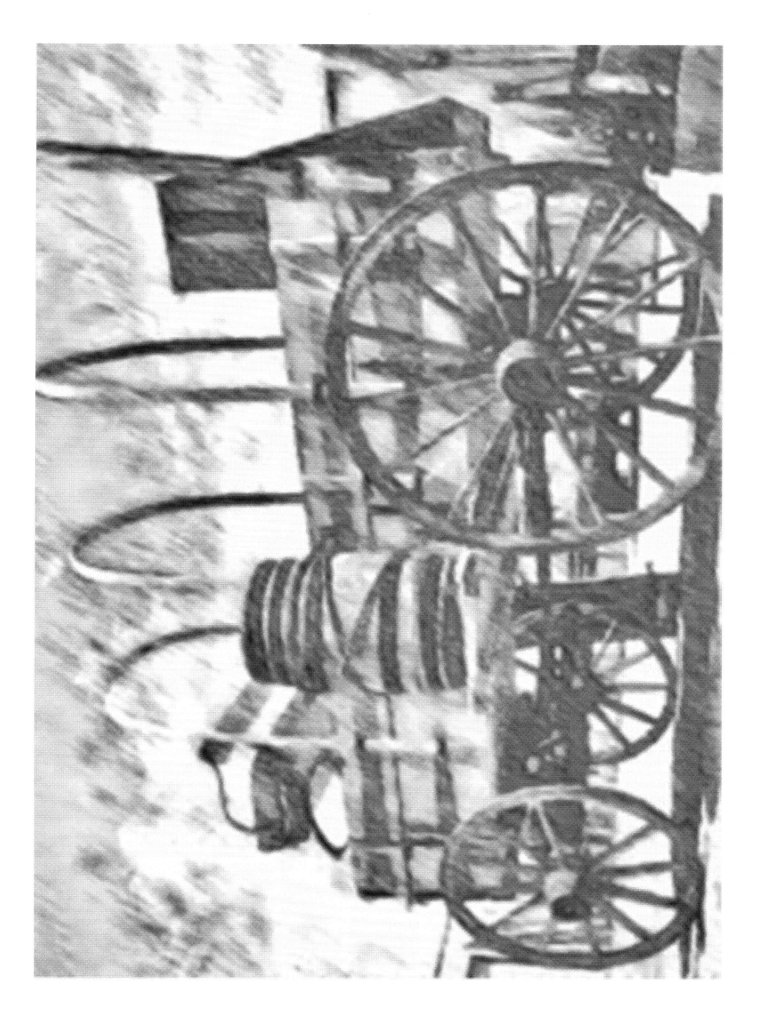

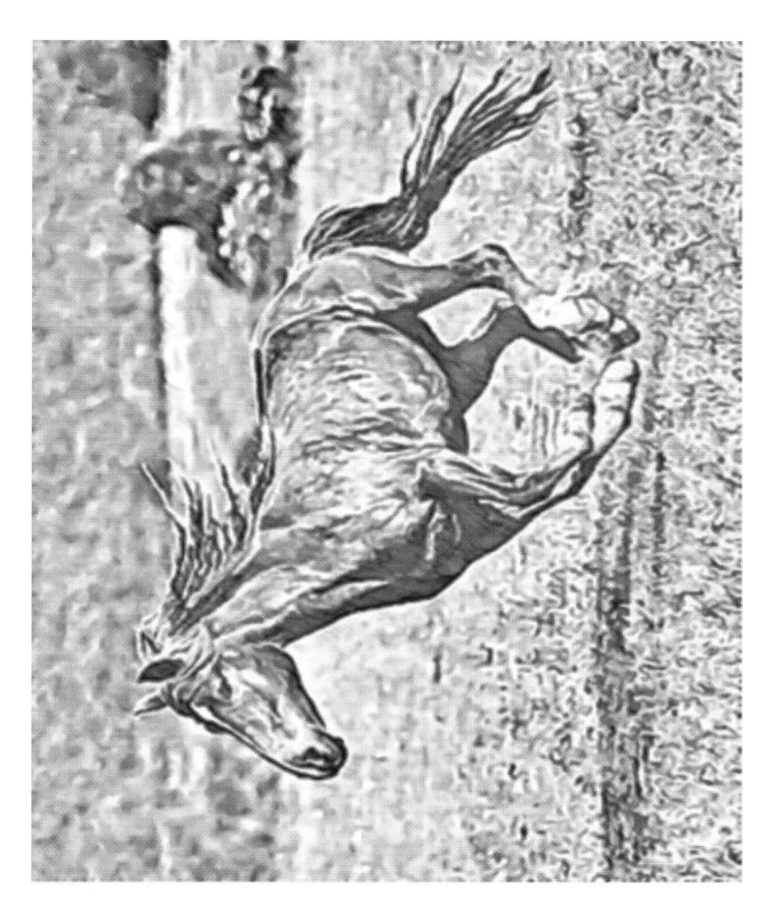

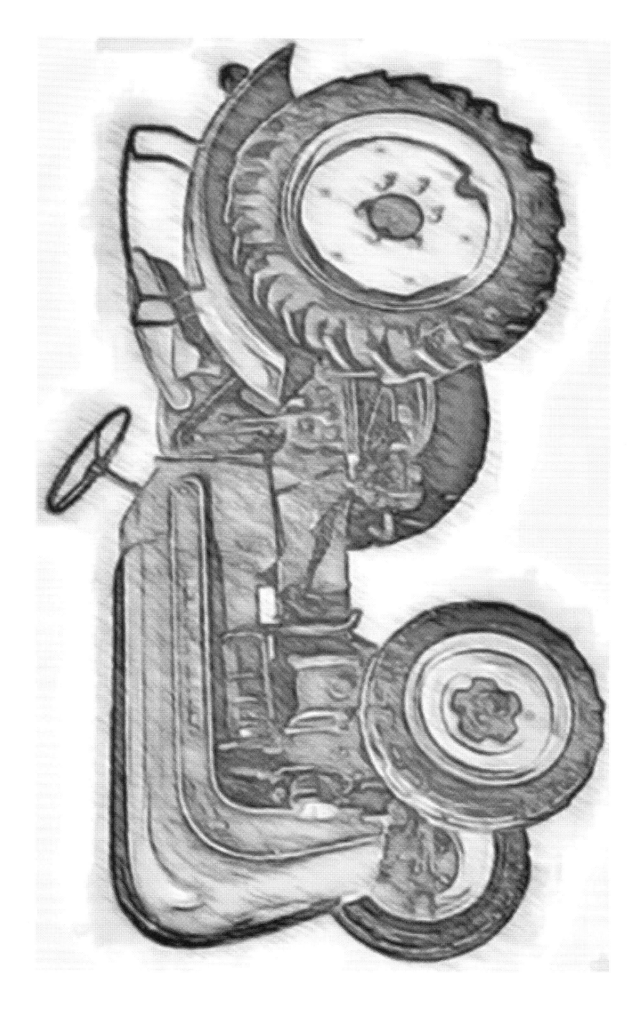

Made in the USA
Middletown, DE
15 January 2020